First published in the UK in 2020 by
Tyne Bridge Publishing, City Library,
Newcastle-upon-Tyne, United Kingdom
www.tynebridgepublishing.org.uk

Copyright © 2020 The Newcastle upon Tyne Hospitals NHS Foundation Trust

All rights reserved. No part of this publication may be reproduced, stored in a retrieval system or transmitted, in any form or by any means, electronic, mechanical, recording or otherwise, in any part of the world, without the prior written permission of the copyright holder.

The right of Philippa Gaunt to be identified as the author of this work has been asserted by her in accordance with Sections 77 and 78 of the Copyright, Design and Patents Act 1988.

This book is sold subject to the condition that it shall not, by way of trade or otherwise, be lent, resold, hired out, or otherwise circulated without the publisher's prior consent in any form of binding or cover other than that in which it is published and without a similar condition, including this condition, being imposed on the subsequent purchaser.

Artwork: Sarah Dickson

ISBN- 13: 978-0-9503178-8-5

# THE great north CHILDREN'S HOSPITAL foundation

Newcastle upon Tyne Hospitals NHS Charity (reg.1057213)

Beyond the warm and dusty sands,
Before land meets the seas,
Lies a big and leafy jungle,
Hiding animals in the trees.

The animals are big and small,
And live in harmony,
But when they are most unwell,
A doctor they must see.

To hospital the animals go,
To meet a great big team.
The doctors, nurses, everyone,
Make it work like a dream.

So let us join the medical team,
And find out who they'll meet.
Those sitting in the waiting room,
With them, let's take a seat!

# How to use this book

This story hopes to help you understand about a medical condition called **asthma**. Some of the words in bold you may not have heard of before but don't worry. You can look up the words in the **glossary** at the back of the book. We hope you enjoy the story!

The content of this book has been reviewed by Paediatric Respiratory Specialists and aims to be as factually accurate as possible.

# Hatty the Hyena

Hatty the Hyena is waiting to be seen.

For days she has been coughing,
with no rest in between.

"I cough and I splutter,
all through the day and night."

"I've been coughing
very loudly and
everyone gets a fright."

"I can barely say full words,
when I try to run."

"All I want is to get well,
so I can have some fun!"

"Usually my asthma is well under control,
when I take my inhalers I feel I'm on a roll!"

My Inhaler and Spacer

My Asthma Plan

My Peak Flow

My Brown and Blue Inhaler

I see my team often so that they can review,
the use of my inhalers; the brown one and the blue."

"I used my blue inhaler to try and help me to breathe. But after 10 big puffs, my breathing did not ease."

"I knew that no improvement meant that I was unwell. So quickly I did find a grown up I could tell."

The doctor looked very closely, at Hatty's deep breaths in.

And counted every time that she sucked her chest out and in.

He noted that she was, breathing really quite fast. And despite the **blue inhaler** her symptoms still did last.

He took his doctor's stethoscope
and placed it on her chest.

He listened very closely,
and told her just to rest.

"When I listen in," he said

"I can hear lots of WHEEZE

It may have just been triggered

by a cool jungle

Although it is the jungle,

it can be COLD at night

And changes in the weather,

can make your chest feel

There could be other triggers that can make you feel ill.
So think right back, to the start, were you climbing a hill?"

"Sometimes, it can be pets or dust right up your nose.

Sometimes, it can be wearing wet fur or soggy clothes.

Or climbing over boulders, running very fast too!

Can make you reach for your, inhaler that is blue."

Hatty simply could not think what caused symptoms this time. She avoided all her triggers and generally felt fine.

When checking over Hatty,
her oxygen was low
and so she needed medicines,
before she could go.

"Let's use a nebuliser,
to open up your airways.
The mask can be quite noisy,
but do not be afraid."

"We'll check again quite shortly,
when medicine has gone through.
When we know your chest is clear,
We'll say goodbye to you."

The nebuliser started, with a gigantic

Medicine 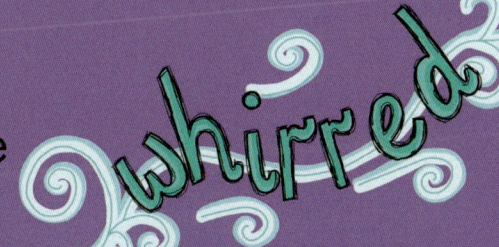 up Hatty's nose

 and  and

The treatment worked its magic,
Hatty soon felt much better.
Getting up and about because
medicine now let her.

As the day went on and on,
treatment was used much less.
Once four hours had passed by,
the doctors felt success

had been achieved with treatment and a well-controlled wean. Hatty felt that she was now the best that she had been.

She did not need her oxygen, and was back on her inhalers. Hatty felt so happy that treatment was not a failure

Soon she had recovered and was back on her feet. The team checked Hatty had good inhaler technique.

Step 1

Step 2

Step 3

They checked that she knew how to use all her inhalers, remembering to always use inhalers with her spacer.

The team told her again the signs that she may see that mean that she should seek some help quite urgently.

- ☑ Breathing very quickly,
- ☑ A chest that feels too tight,
- ☑ No relief with inhalers that should help day and night.

Once the team were happy,
Hatty was good to go.
In control of her wheeze,
the team had reached their goal!

Hatty knew now how to spot when her asthma was bad and when to see a doctor who may decide to add…

My Blue and Brown Inhalers

My Inhalers attached to a Spacer

Treatment with a Nebuliser

…other treatments that may help Hatty to breathe with ease so her chest will sound clear without any loud wheeze.

Hatty left the hospital and headed straight for home, knowing that her asthma would allow her still to roam the jungle with her friends who knew the warning signs so they could help Hatty if needed in good time.

Hatty felt much happier knowing that she could play and that asthma would not stop her living life her way!

# Glossary

**Asthma** — A disease which makes airways (tubes) in your lungs narrow, making it difficult to breathe. It can feel like breathing through a straw.

**Asthma Plan** — A plan written by doctors and nurses for children with asthma that tells you what medicines to take in an asthma attack and when to go to hospital. Your plan is unique to you.

**Blue Inhaler (reliever)** — Salbutamol (Sal-boo-ta-mol) medicine that children take when they feel their chest getting tight and it becomes difficult to breathe. Some children take this inhaler before exercise to stop them from getting wheezy.

**Brown Inhaler (preventer)** — Medicine that children take regularly to stop their airways becoming narrow.

**Inhaler(s)** — The device used to give you the medicines used to treat asthma. There are lots of different types and colours!

**Inhaler Technique** — The steps followed so that when using your inhaler, you get all of your medicine.

**Nebuliser** — A mask in which medicine is mixed in with oxygen so it can enter the airways and make them less tight and narrow, helping you to breathe. This is used when your oxygen levels are low.

**Oxygen** — A gas in the air that enters our body when we breathe in and that we need to help the body work. When airways are narrow, sometimes it's difficult to get oxygen into the body.

| | |
|---|---|
| **Peak Flow** | A tube into which you try and blow as hard as you can. This helps the team measure how well controlled your asthma is. Some children keep a diary of these measurements. |
| **Spacer** | A device that can be attached to your inhaler to help make sure you breathe in all your inhaler medicine. Should be used with all inhalers. |
| **Stethoscope** | A set of tubes that doctors and nurses use to listen to how you are breathing. |
| **Triggers** | Things that can cause children's airways to get tight and narrow. Everyone has different triggers but this could include dust, pets, exercise, cigarette smoke plus many more! |
| **Wean** | When doctors and nurses try to spread out how often you are given treatment based on how tight you chest feels and whether there is a wheeze. |
| **Wheeze** | The breathing sound often heard when a child is having a flare of their asthma. |

For more information on asthma, please visit the beat asthma website: www.beatasthma.co.uk